Your Fu In a Cup

Channeling
with
Coffee Grounds
A Beginner's Guide to Divination

Magzcha Westerman, M.A.

Note for Librarians: a cataloguing record for this book that includes Dewey Decimal Classification and US Library of Congress numbers is available from the Library and Archives of Canada. The complete cataloguing record can be obtained from their online database at:
www.collectionscanada.ca/amicus/index-e.html
ISBN 1-4120-5055-3
Printed in Victoria, BC, Canada

TRAFFORD

Offices in Canada, USA, Ireland, UK and Spain
This book was published *on-demand* in cooperation with Trafford Publishing. On-demand publishing is a unique process and service of making a book available for retail sale to the public taking advantage of on-demand manufacturing and Internet marketing. On-demand publishing includes promotions, retail sales, manufacturing, order fulfilment, accounting and collecting royalties on behalf of the author.
Book sales for North America and international:
Trafford Publishing, 6E–2333 Government St.,
Victoria, BC v8t 4p4 CANADA
phone 250 383 6864 (toll-free 1 888 232 4444)
fax 250 383 6804; email to orders@trafford.com
Book sales in Europe:
Trafford Publishing (uk) Ltd., Enterprise House, Wistaston Road Business Centre,
Wistaston Road, Crewe, Cheshire cw2 7rp UNITED KINGDOM
phone 01270 251 396 (local rate 0845 230 9601)
facsimile 01270 254 983; orders.uk@trafford.com
Order online at:
www.trafford.com/robots/04-2863.html

10 9 8 7 6

CONTENTS

DEDICATION

To The Reverend Saul Weiss, a compassionate, generous, gifted and powerful healer. Now in the world of spirit, his memory lives on and continues to inspire and heal.

ACKNOWLEDGMENTS

My deep and everlasting gratitude goes to those teachers and guides "in spirit," who helped and inspired me throughout this endeavor. Although not personally known to me, I am aware of their presence , and believe they are responsible for forming the remarkable and artistically beautiful images in the grounds.

A very special and loving thanks to my Native American spirit guide, "*Big Eagle*," who periodically leaves the unmistakable image of an eagle in my grounds, just to remind me of his ongoing care and assistance.

Thanks also to Drs. Paul and Barbara Daniele, founders of the College of Metaphysical Studies in Clearwater, Florida, for inviting me to participate in their psychic festivals, where I photographed some of the coffee ground images found within these pages.

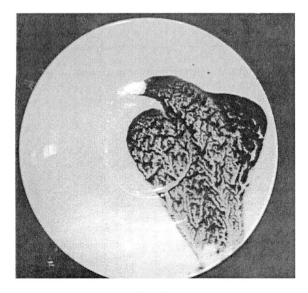

Eagle

LIST OF ILLUSTRATIONS

PREFACE

Handed down from mother to daughter through the centuries, the ancient art of channeling with coffee grounds continues to be widely practiced throughout the Middle East, North Africa, Turkey, Greece and other Balkan States.

Many years ago, a Moroccan friend taught me the rudiments of this fascinating tradition, and I've been peering into expresso cups ever since. Each time, I am opened anew to a world of mystery and magic. People, animals, spirit guides, angels, messengers and messages regularly appear in my own and others' cups.

Channeling with coffee grounds ("cup reading") is a method of divining past, present, and future from images formed in the grounds. It is a process which promotes the ability to visualize and concentrate. More importantly, it will expand your consciousness by opening doors to worlds beyond our own, to unseen dimensions of existence.

The following pages provide a thorough but simple step-by-step approach to a very old practice, one which allows you to actually see into the near future. If you pursue this form of divination, you will embark upon an exciting journey of discovery and adventure. Surprises are in store, not the least of which is the enjoyment of a delicious and exotic cup of coffee.

SECTION I

THE TEXT

Chapters 1 through 10

Chapter 1

INTRODUCTION

CHANNELING

Diviners, psychics, channelers, readers, counselors, advisors–however we choose to describe ourselves–are conduits, or channels–for the information and guidance which flow through us, and which come from a dimension beyond the earth plane. Whether from spirit guides, angels, one's own "high self" or some other source, a degree of channeling is at work when we divine for others.

Channeling can be an intentional and completely conscious process, or it can be a completely unconscious process. Many people are unaware of their own participation in this process. Take, for example, the mom who always "knows" when her children are in danger. Is she channeling a warning from a guardian angel, or perhaps tapping into a unified field wherein everything and everyone are connected? She receives psychic insights, but is not concerned with the how or why of it.

DIVINATION

Divination is the act of receiving and revealing information about the past, present or future. This information is channeled through the diviner either directly, or through tools such as tarot cards, rune stones, tea leaves or coffee grounds, etc.

While divining from coffee grounds involves a degree of channeling, not all channelers actually divine, or foretell events. Mediums, for example, can communicate with the departed. They channel messages of hope and comfort from "the other side" to bereaved relatives and friends.

Other channelers utilize a trance state in order to allow an entity, usually a highly developed "being of light" to speak through them. The entity may use its host's vocal chords to communicate spiritual teachings to humanity.

PROPHESY

Prophets make predictions of things to come as if by divine inspiration. What is the difference between a prophet and a diviner? Very little, except in scope. Prophets tend to predict events of great magnitude, while diviners commonly limit their predictions to more immediate and personal matters.

THE "SLEEPING PROPHET"

The American seer, Edgar Cayce, renowned for his healing abilities, channeled his information while in a self-induced hypnotic trance. He was able to diagnose his clients' physical illnesses from a great distance, but could also perceive their past lives and prescribe the necessary treatments for healing both body and soul.

Known as the "Sleeping Prophet," Cayce shed light on many historical figures and prophesied many future events. His "readings" were meticulously documented, and can be found at the Association for Research and Enlightenment in Virginia Beach. Cayce not only channeled, but he divined and prophesied as well. His powers were extraordinary, as is the large body of his work.

AS A BEGINNER ...

Unlike the Cayce's of this world, you are a novice, a beginning psychic, so don't expect to foresee events of great significance. At best, you may hone in on your subject's immediate present, recent past, and near future. As you progress in your studies and gain experience, your vision will expand.

CLAIRVOYANTS, CLAIRAUDIENTS, CLAIRSENTIENTS

Channeled information is usually received in one or more of the following ways:

Clairvoyants receive their information through sight, by seeing images in their minds;

Clairaudients hear voices and/or other sounds; and *Clairsentients* receive their information through physical sensations.

Some psychics just have a strong sense of knowing, or may experience any or all of the above in combination.

Reading coffee grounds, however, requires yet another ability; the ability to visualize forms and images from the grounds in a cup.

VISUALIZING IMAGES

Interpreting the grounds in a cup depends upon the presence of visual images and the reader's ability to see them. When coffee and cup are properly prepared, pictures are actually formed by the grounds. The thick, sweet expresso of the Middle East, Greece, Turkey, etc., so different from American coffee, is a perfect vehicle for divination.

The powdered grounds are cooked right into the coffee, so they settle at the bottom of the cup while the coffee is being sipped off the top. When the coffee has been drunk, the petit expresso cup is turned upside down. The syrupy grounds at the bottom of the cup drip down the inside of the cup, forming pictures along the way. When the dripping has stopped, the cup is turned back upright, and the diviner "reads" the pictures in the grounds. ***Saucer images*** also provide a rich source of imagery for divination. They are formed when the coffee left in the saucer is poured off.

IMAGE ORIGINS

Where do these images come from? How do they arise? Are they nothing more than random, accidental patterns? Are they formed by one's own psycho-kinetic energy, or plucked, perhaps, from a universal memory bank and projected onto the grounds in a cup or saucer? Could spirit guides or angels be sending us messages via images in coffee grounds?

IMAGES IN SAUCER GROUNDS

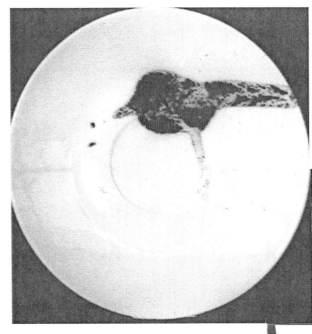

Beast of burden (?)
wearing a saddle.

Bird
Birds are messengers, carrying messages, but specific birds carry more specific messages. A bird at rest brings a fortunate message.

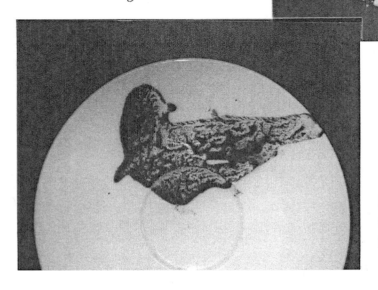

Otter
Life has become too serious and burdensome. Learn to play again.

THE COLLECTIVE UNCONSCIOUS

While some of the images formed by the grounds are visible only to the diviner, others are as beautifully defined as a photograph or painting, and clearly seen by everyone who looks at them. These images are not limited to the eyes of the beholder. Many of them have appeared recurringly throughout history and in diverse cultures; in dreams, myths, folk and fairy tales, religion, etc., and seem to live in a timeless realm of their own.

This realm is known as *The Collective Unconscious,* a term coined by Carl Gustav Jung, father of Jungian psychology. Jung believed that some portion of the unconscious mind is universal; that its contents are more or less the same everywhere and in all individuals. That may explain why so many symbols have the same or similar interpretations across different cultures.

SPIRIT GUIDES?

A spirit guide is a guardian teacher who once was alive and lived among men. Having made a transition to another plane of existence, or, as Native Americans say "the spirit world," the guide takes on the responsibility of helping and teaching those of us on earth. Many cultures believe in the existence of spirit guides, and Native Americans in particular believe that we all have them.

My *personal* experience has led me to believe that, in some way and to some extent, spirit guides *may* be responsible for the formation of the images in coffee grounds, and for the insights we have while interpreting them. Perhaps they are able to tap into the collective unconscious; perhaps they are a part of it.

Your experience may lead you to a different conclusion, for the ways in which information from other dimensions is received, transmitted, interpreted and communicated to others, are as diverse as individual diviners themselves.

Chapter 2

GETTING STARTED

BEFORE PROCEEDING, CONSIDER THE FOLLOWING:

1. Channeling opens a door to the beyond, through which may enter energies from other dimensions such as the "astral plane," a vast region somewhere between heaven and earth. It is important, therefore, that you allow only wise counsel to be channeled through you and that you strive to be a sincere spiritual vehicle for that counsel. Prayer and meditation are simple and effective tools which will assist you in achieving that goal.

2. If you are physically ill, emotionally distressed, or going through a psychologically difficult time, using drugs, alcohol or mood altering medications of any kind, including antidepressants or tranquilizers, postpone the cup reading for another time. *Positive energy* is essential to success.

3. Ideally, a person who counsels others will have tact, diplomacy, and even the uncanny ability to anticipate a subject's emotional reaction to the information being communicated.

In short, you need to have (or to develop) the kind of sensitivity which will enable you to transmit information in an intelligent, honest, but discretionary and helpful manner. The *way* in which you communicate, especially when dealing with delicate issues, is as important as *what* you communicate. You hold the power to comfort or frighten. Can you use it wisely?

If you have considered these factors and are ready to continue, then the guidelines presented throughout these pages will pave the way for the development of your divinatory talents and open you to the magic of mystical experience.

FORM A GROUP

Learning the art of reading grounds takes time and practice. An effective way to gain and share experience is within a small group. Participants take turns examining the same cup, describing what they see, and offering interpretations. A diversity of cups and the input and feedback coming from others enhances the learning process.

Within a group, only one cup at a time should be looked at and studied; all other participants' cups await their respective turns. Reading more than one cup at a time—even looking at another cup silently—scatters the psychic energy within the group and interferes with the reading.

If a group is not available to you (just one or two others would suffice), then practice with people who will give you the opportunity to nurture your talent and hone your communication skills by providing honest feedback and constructive criticism.

SET A MOOD

The degree to which you successfully channel via coffee grounds directly reflects your state of mind. Before proceeding, all negativity must be released and the cares of the day dissolved. Anger, frustration or fatigue will impair your ability to read.

Therefore, start by creating an atmosphere in which you can totally relax and fill yourself with peace and positive energy. Some readers set a mood with candles, incense, music, crystals, etc., while others just sit quietly in meditation or prayer.

GUARD THE DOOR

While divination is believed by some to result only from contact with divine-like energies, opening a door to the beyond extends an invitation, and **_anything_** can step through that door if permitted to do so.

For that reason, you should learn how to ground and protect yourself *before using any form of divination.* "Grounding" connects and roots you to the earth, whose energy is stabilizing, secure and protective. Prayer, of course, is always powerfully protective.

If you don't know how to ground and protect yourself, you may find the following meditation helpful.

WHITE LIGHT AND GROUNDING MEDITATION

1. Sit in a comfortable chair, eyes closed, feet flat on the floor with hands in lap, palms up.

2. Breathe deeply, inhaling through your nose and exhaling through your mouth, until your breathing becomes slow and regular. Continue breathing in this manner and allow yourself to relax completely.

3. Imagine that with each inhalation, you are breathing in a white light vibration of love, peace and protection. Imagine this light circulating throughout your body, touching every cell, and purifying, healing and protecting you as it does so.

4. With each exhalation, breathe out all negativity, anger, frustration, fatigue and illness. Imagine these negative energies being dispersed into the cosmos, where they are cleansed, purified, and transformed into positive energy.

5. Continue to breathe in this manner, inhaling the white light of love, peace and protection, and exhaling all negative thought and emotion. Imagine the light extending out from your body, surrounding you with a protective, impenetrable shield.

6. Your breathing in the light and exhaling negativity is, by now, automatic. No need to think about it; your breathing in this manner will continue of its own accord. It's time now to start the grounding part of this meditation.

GROUNDING

7. Imagine yourself in a place of beauty, surrounded by nature, your feet planted firmly on the soil of Mother Earth. Can you feel the damp, cool green grass beneath your feet, between your toes? Can you smell the fresh, fertile fragrance of the vegetation around you? Imagine your feet growing roots which extend deep down into the bowels of the earth, as if your legs were the trunk of a sturdy old tree. You are now solidly grounded in the earth, ready to receive its nurturing, stabilizing, protective care.

8. Allow that earth energy to pour into you through the roots of your feet, and to circulate up into and throughout your body.

9. Bring together the white light of heaven and the stabilizing, protective energy of earth, mingling them throughout your body, until these energies are comfortably balanced. Take as much time as you need.

10. When you are ready to leave your meditative state and return to your present surroundings, draw your roots back up into your feet, retaining your invisible connection to the earth.

11. Close your meditation with a prayer. Ask again for protection both for yourself and for your subject. If you believe that you are being assisted in your process, add a thank you for the blessing you've received as a messenger with the gift of divination.

You are now protected, grounded, and ready to receive and communicate only the wisest counsel for the highest good of your subject.

RECOMMENDATION

If you wish to utilize this meditation and cannot initially remember it, record it. Play it back each time you are about to commence divining, following the instructions along with the recording. Eventually, you will no longer need to do this; you will be able to meditate and pray without assistance.

Chapter 3

SUPPLIES AND PREPARATION

CUP AND SAUCER

THE POT

THE COFFEE

Historically, coffee grounds are read with powdered coffee known as "Greek" or "Turkish" expresso. It is available at Greek and Middle Eastern grocery shops. If unavailable, purchase some whole beans at your local super market and grind the beans on the setting marked "Turkish." This coffee will not be as finely powdered as Greek or Turkish coffee, but will suffice until you can obtain the commercial powdered coffee.

CUP AND SAUCER

Use a demitasse cup or petit tea cup. It must be solid white on the inside, without decorations; is preferably wider at the rim than at the base; has a handle; and a solid white saucer to accompany it. The saucer should be smooth, not grooved.

THE POT

The traditional ethnic pot used for preparing powdered coffee has a long handle and pointed tip on the rim to facilitate pouring, but any small saucepan can be used instead.

PREPARING THE COFFEE

This coffee must be served black; milk or cream will "muddy" the grounds and interfere with a reading.

1.　　Pour one demitasse cup of water ***for each serving*** into the pot.

2.　　Add to the water one slightly rounded teaspoon of powdered coffee and one level teaspoon of sugar or sugar substitute ***for each serving.***

3.　　Bring to a boil and remove the pot from the heat immediately, or the coffee will foam up and overflow the pot. Bring to a boil two more times (a total of three times) in succession, until a frothy foam is formed.

　　It is said that there is something magical about the number three, but in any case, that is the way it is done in the Middle East.

4.   Stir the coffee before pouring it into each cup. This assures that the grounds, which sink to the bottom of the pot, will be evenly distributed in all the cups.

5.   Pour each cup only one-half full, stir the coffee in the pot again, and then complete the pouring process by going around to each cup a second time.

BEFORE DRINKING

Before drinking the coffee, each cup should be allowed to sit untouched for a few minutes. This gives the powdered grounds a chance to sink to the bottom of the cup, leaving the clearer, grounds-free liquid at the top.

During these few minutes, keep your hand on the cup. Why? Your touch will add more of your personal vibration. You might wish to silently think about what you would like to know. This time can also be used to thank your helpers for their assistance (this would be in addition to the longer process of meditation or prayer which preceded the entire process).

DRINKING THE COFFEE

The coffee has been poured and served; the grounds have settled to the bottom of each cup; and the coffee is now ready to drink.

1.   Sip the coffee gently off the top of the cup without shaking the cup. This keeps the grounds at the bottom.

2.   Do not drink all the coffee; leave about a teaspoon of the liquid at the bottom, covering the grounds. If you can't drink that much coffee, pour some off into a sink or bowl.

3.   Gently stir together the coffee and grounds at the bottom of the cup to form a syrupy consistency. The cup is now ready to be turned upside-down.

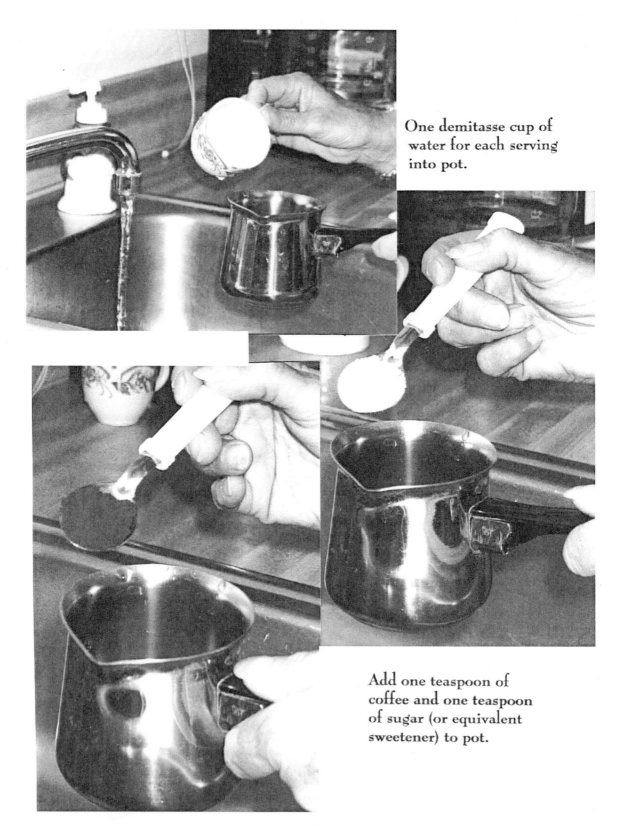

One demitasse cup of
water for each serving
into pot.

Add one teaspoon of
coffee and one teaspoon
of sugar (or equivalent
sweetener) to pot.

Bring to a boil and remove from heat. Do this three times. Stir the coffee in the pot to assure equal distribution of the grounds. Fill each cup ½ full, stir again, and finish pouring.

INVERTING THE CUP (see illustrations, page 17)

The reason for inverting the cup is that the syrupy coffee at the bottom of the cup will drip down the sides of the upside-down cup, forming images along the way. It is these images which are eventually "read" when the dripping grounds have dried and the cup returned to its upright position. Each cup must be handled and turned *only* by the person drinking from it.

1.   Place the saucer, face down, on top of the upright cup.

2.   Holding the saucer firmly over the cup with both hands, turn them both upside-down in one movement. The saucer will catch the excess coffee.

3.   While the cup is still upside-down, and *without turning it upright*, lift slightly from the saucer and pour the excess coffee from the saucer into a sink or bowl.

     Images may be formed in the saucer as the coffee is being poured off it.

4.   Place the still inverted cup, rim down, onto the edge of the saucer. This position allows air to get up inside, facilitating the drying process.

     Leave the cup in this position for about five minutes, giving the grounds ample time to stop dripping and to dry.

     Do not turn or move the cup during this time.

5.   When the coffee inside the cup has stopped dripping and the grounds are dry, turn the cup upright. It is now ready to be read.

The following chapter will describe what you are likely to see upon turning the cup upright.

INVERTING THE CUP

First

Second

Third

Fourth

Place saucer on top of cup. Using both hands, turn them both upside down at once. Saucer will catch excess coffee.

Lift cup without turning it, and pour excess coffee into sink. Replace cup over edge of saucer, allowing the grounds to dry.

Chapter 4

THE GROUNDS WILL SHOW ...

GENERAL PATTERNS

When a cup is returned to its upright position for reading, one of the first things seen is the general pattern formed by the grounds. While no two cups are ever the same, some common patterns repeatedly emerge.

1. Grounds so light and sparce they are hardly visible. This results from too much liquid remaining in the cup before it is inverted. ***The grounds are too diluted.***

2. Many crowded images spread around the entire inside of the cup. This can result from ***too much shaking or movement of the cup*** before it is inverted.

3. One or more groupings of images which take on recognizable shapes. ***This pattern is ideal for reading.***

4. A large clump of grounds, either by itself or with other images nearby. This can result from inadequate mixing of the grounds and liquid at the bottom of the cup before it was inverted.

    However, that clump is sometimes an integral part of the message, symbolizing an obstacle, problem or challenge to be overcome. Nearby images may shed light on the meaning of the formation.

TYPES OF IMAGES

With regard to the pictures formed by the grounds, there is no way of knowing beforehand what you will see. Nevertheless, the following types of images seem to appear more frequently than others:

FREQUENTLY APPEARING IMAGES.

ANIMALS: Animal images appear frequently. While usually

18

GENERAL PATTERNS

Too much liquid, not
enough grounds.

Too much shaking of the cup
before it was inverted.

The Clump
An obstacle, problem or chal-
lenge to be overcome.

One large grouping of images.

EXPECT THE UNEXPECTED

African Antelope

Spirit Guide Face?

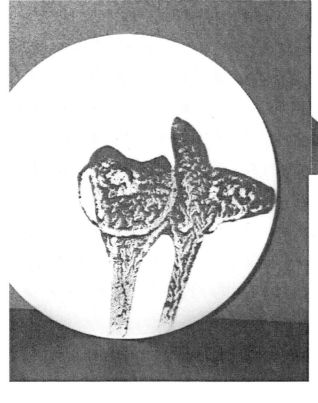

Shark (facing up) and woman's face in semi-circle. What do you see?

interpreted symbolically, they can also be taken literally.

Symbolically, a dog represents "a friend." However, the dog's picture in the grounds may literally refer to the subject's real pet.

Animals sometimes symbolize people who share their characteristics. An alligator, for example, means "a thick-skinned person"; a lion is "a powerful person in authority"; a beaver represents "a builder," and so on.

Animals may also symbolize abstract concepts. A dove means "peace"; an ermine means "purity" (because it is white).

PEOPLE: Human figures and faces show up frequently, and are usually interpreted literally. That is, ***people represent people***. A specific person can sometimes be recognized from appearance, or from something close by, such as an initial or astrological symbol. If an unrecognized person appears in the grounds, it may refer to someone presently unknown but coming into the subject's life.

Sometimes, however, a figure with a recognizable nationality (as for example, a Spanish bull fighter) can refer to a place. The subject may be considering a trip to that location, or have relatives, friends, business or some other connection there.

COLUMNS: These are medium to long, slender, sometimes serpentine, columns. They usually indicate trips, but may also symbolize a chosen path or journey of the mind.

Commencing at the bottom of the cup, the column extending up to the rim may signify a long journey. If it terminates before reaching the rim–or perhaps half-way up the cup–then it may refer to a shorter trip. The longer the column, the longer the journey. It must be noted, however, that for people who rarely travel or leave their homes (elderly, disabled, etc.), what appears to be a long trip may be nothing more than a short trip to the super market.

Sometimes, figures, faces or other images appear within a column, touching it or next to it. These may shed light upon the circumstances of the trip (destination, others involved, etc.)

OCCASIONAL IMAGES

CHILDREN AND BABIES: Children and babies occasionally appear in cups, and have both literal and symbolic meanings. A child's image can refer to a specific child in the subject's life (literal interpretation), or it can symbolize "an unnecessary expense" (symbolic interpretation).

An infant or baby can refer to a specific infant or baby, but could also symbolize "the birth of a new project." A fetus can signify an actual pregnancy, but it, too, can represent "the birth of a new project."

SPIRIT GUIDES AND ANGELS: Spirit guides appear in cups only rarely, and can usually be distinguished from living people by appearance; in the case of angels, by their wings.

Throughout the history of religious art, angels have been depicted with feathered wings, predetermining our expectation of their appearance. Strangely, however, the angels seen by me, my students and clients, do not have feathered wings as traditionally portrayed. Rather, they are delicate and diaphanous, like butterfly wings.

Can anyone really know where reality, expectation and imagination merge when dealing with dimensions beyond what our limited senses can discern? Probably not, but you will know an angel when you see one.

NUMBERS AND WORDS: Numbers appear more frequently than words. They can refer to almost anything: a calendar date; a month of the year; a time of day; or something of personal significance known only to the subject.

Words appear quite rarely, and speak for themselves. Once, the name *Reuben* mysteriously appeared in the grounds at the bottom of my student's cup. It was the name of a deceased relative. Was this a message from someone in spirit?

DOTS, DASHES AND OTHER SHAPES: Dots, dashes, and some geometrical forms have traditional interpretations in cup reading:

Dots: Money

Dashes: Projects in the works; enterprises afoot

Wavy lines: Uncertainty; unsettlement

Triangles: Good luck if apex is pointed up; disappointment
                   if pointed down

Squares: Protection

Arrows: Bad news

There are numerous other shapes which periodically appear, in addition to the endless number of image types not mentioned in this chapter. Their interpretations might be found in Section II, but if not, do some research. Seek out books on symbols (see bibliography), and continue to expand your symbolic vocabulary.

Chapter 5

THE MESSAGES

MEANINGFUL MESSAGES:

Despite the unpredictability of what can be seen in any cup, the information conveyed by the grounds usually falls into two categories, meaningful or unimportant junk mail. A meaningful message informs and carries purposeful, significant information. Here is an example from my files:

> The grounds revealed the image of an angel hovering over a very old and sickly woman, implying an impending transition with the help of angelic presence. This message regarding a beloved grandmother was particularly meaningful to my client. It helped prepare her for the forthcoming event in a comforting and reassuring way.

JUNK MAIL:

Insignificant information can appear as many small or unrecognizable shapes scattered around a cup. The grounds have formed few, if any, clear-cut images. I call this "junk mail."

Junk Mail

If an entire cup is filled with junk mail, one of several things may be happening:

1. The cup may be reflecting the subject's unfocused state of mind.
2. The subject's life may be very busy but nothing of consequence is happening at that time.
3. The cup may be reflecting the diviner's inability to channel at that time.
4. Or, the cup may have been shaken or turned incorrectly.

The best thing to do in such a situation is to explain the possible reasons for such a cup and suggest another reading at a later date. If a cup contains both good sized, well defined images **and** junk mail, concentrate on the readable images; these are the ones conveying messages.

WARNING SYMBOLS:

Messages sometimes come as warnings. These can be warnings of physical danger, illness, deception, etc. There are many warning symbols which appear in cups. Among those which I have seen most frequently and across cultures, are: a cross (illness); a black spot on a part of the body (illness of that part of the body); an owl (deception, failure, danger, etc.); a mouse (theft); a toad (false flatterer); and a bat (a pointless task or fruitless journey).

Do we respond to such images with apprehension or gratitude? Take the owl, for example.

OWL: SINISTER OMEN OR WISE COUNSEL?

There was a time when the appearance of an owl in the grounds caused me apprehension. Being inexperienced, I had not yet reconciled the difference between the owl as a very ancient symbol of wisdom, and the owl as a sinister omen.

However, in researching the owl's mythology, I discovered that it was the companion bird of Athena, Greek warrior goddess and protectress of Athens. Athena's many attributes and responsibilities also included her role as a goddess of wisdom and prophesy.   Thus, the owl's association with both wisdom and prophesy.

In European and Anglo-American folklore, the owl is often portrayed as a bird of ill omen. Native American tradition holds two opposing views. There are those who abhor the bird as an omen of great evil, its image banned from tribal grounds. Others perceive it as a messenger come to warn of danger, and therefore a welcome friend/protector.

The wisdom aspects of owl see beyond the light of day and into the mystery of night. They come to caution us with prophetic vision when danger is at hand and a warning is required.

What, after all, is the purpose of reading cups, if not to receive messages?   Of hope, encouragement, advice, and ***also of caution***. Warnings come as sage counsel from a source of love and caring for our well-being. It is the wise reader who respects and heeds the messages of "wise old owl" and other precautionary omens.

Owl Head, Fish Body, Scorpion's Tail
Combined image warns of financial woes (fish means money), owl brings bad luck, and scorpion stings. Put them together and you have a warning regarding money matters.

Scorpion
"Beware the scorpion's sting!"

WARNING SYMBOLS

Water Monster
Appeared just prior to Hurricane
George. Look for the small trident,
symbol of Neptune, God of the Sea,
on the handle side of the image.

Giraffe
Mischief brewing.

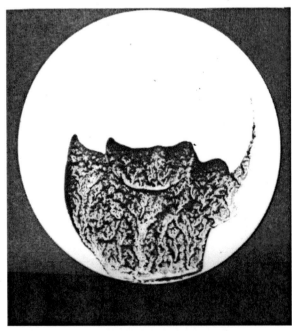

Combined Image of Bat-Owl
Bat--A worthless journey, a fruitless task.
Owl-Bad luck, failure, danger, deception.
Message—Don't make that trip.

Boot and Shoe
The kick-out.
Getting "the boot."

GROUPED WARNINGS:

In addition to the individual warning symbols mentioned above, there are other kinds of "be careful" messages which do not appear as single images. Sometimes, a pattern of related images contains a warning *theme.*

A student of mine had a cup showing nothing but water images, most of which seemed relatively benign, except for two–a large jellyfish and a "Siren." (In Greek mythology, Sirens are the sea nymphs whose irresistably seductive song lured unwary sailors to their deaths. Ulysses is said to have escaped them by plugging the ears of his crew with wax).

Since Ann was about to take a Caribbean Island vacation, I cautioned her against water activities in favor of others, and advised her to carefully monitor the weather. When Hurricane Luis came along, Ann was on an early flight home to safety.

EXPANDING YOUR SYMBOLIC VOCABULARY:

Symbols derive not only from mythology, dreams, folk tales and religion, etc., but also from historic and contemporary literature, as well as life itself.

For example, two books, *The Medicine Cards* and *Animal Speak* (see bibliography), both written from a Native American perspective, have been of invaluable help with the interpretation of certain animal images seen in the grounds.

As our computerized technology spreads and accelerates, so too may its symbols eventually become part of that vast, universal memory bank known as "The Collective Unconscious." While I haven't yet seen a computer in the grounds, airplanes appear frequently, and one client's cup showed a perfectly formed saucer shaped UFO hovering just above a column (trip). The subject had just returned from Mexico City, where UFO sightings are reported to be commonplace.

PERSONAL EXPERIENCE

Personal experience may also increase your symbolic vocabulary. The first time I saw a penguin in my cup, I had no idea what to make of this comical little creature. Shortly thereafter, I was invited to attend a formal affair. Two penguins and two formal affairs later, I added the penguin to my list of symbols to mean "An invitation to a formal affair." The connection between penguins, tuxedos and formal affairs seems quite humorous to me, but whoever said spirit guides lack a sense of humor?

RECORD YOUR OBSERVATIONS:

Each time you observe an image and discover its potential meaning, record it for future testing and application. If you find a meaning for a symbol different from what is listed in Section II, add your discovery to that symbol's traditional meaning.

Nothing here is "written in stone." The art of divining from coffee grounds is an exploratory adventure and an ongoing learning process.

Chapter 6

MIRACULOUS IMAGES

MY FIRST SPIRIT GUIDE

During the initial stages of my work with coffee grounds, the delicately etched image of an elderly, Asian featured man with long, flowing white hair and beard, periodically appeared in my cup.

These were the years prior to my serious participation in the world of metaphysics; before I ever heard of spirit guides, or had any inkling of the existence of such beings. I didn't even know I was channeling. I'd heard the word and knew what it meant, but never associated it with what I personally was doing. Cup reading was just a pleasant pastime, an entertainment for my friends.

Consequently, the old man's reappearing image was always a source of great puzzlement. Who was he? Where was he from, and what was he doing in my cup? After a few years, the image stopped appearing and faded from my memory.

Eventually, my exposure to a variety of metaphysical traditions led me to reflect upon that face, and to speculate that it belonged to a spirit guide. I believed that he had shown himself to me for a purpose: perhaps to elevate my consciousness; perhaps to let me know that I was being gently guided; or perhaps to tell me that it was he who was responsible for the images in my cup; he whose guidance I was channeling–that I had my very own spirit guide, himself.

SPECIAL REQUESTS

When, over time and many years later, these speculations became convictions, I wondered if I might intentionally request the appearance of a guide. So, during a meditation preceding the preparation of my coffee, I asked–without any idea of who or what to expect–that my primary guide appear to me. There, clearly visible in the grounds of my cup was, once again, that same old sage. It was truly a revelation to know that one could request and, indeed, receive.

That experience marked a turning point. Cup reading became a doorway to worlds beyond my known reality, to spirit guides, angels, and more. Since then, I have advised others to ask for what they want to see, and they, too, have sometimes been privileged to receive.

SOMETIMES GRANTED, SOMETIMES NOT

Special requests are sometimes granted, sometimes not. One possible explanation for this is that your guides know better than your conscious mind what you need to know. If a specific request is not relevant to what is truly important, it may be bypassed in favor of information more pertinent to your life at that moment in time.

Another possible reason–experienced by all psychics at one time or another–is that no information at all is received, or that information is received in a way which seems garbled and incomprehensible. We are not all perfect channels all of the time; we are, after all, only human. When I find myself not receiving information clearly, I set aside my divinatory tools and spend some time–days, weeks or even months–centering and balancing myself. I return to cup reading when I am able to receive and accurately interpret what I consider to be information from a sacred source.

It is important to maintain your clarity of mind and purpose; limit your use of the grounds to serious matters, and avoid frivolous issues. When the time is right, your guides will bless you by granting your special requests.

ANGELS

Within my own experience, angels have not appeared when summoned. Yet, they come unbidden. Others, as well as myself, have seen angels in coffee grounds, and their beautiful wings clearly distinguish them from guides and other figures.

Angels reveal themselves for a variety of reasons: to offer a message of hope; sometimes to comfort during times of great stress or during a crisis of faith; and sometimes they appear just to remind us of their presence. Occasionally, the image of an angel will be seen in the grounds hovering next to someone about to make a transition. How comforting it is to know that a loved one has such divine protection, whether that loved one chooses to remain on earth or move on to another dimension of experience.

DEVAS

Animals have angels too. They are sometimes called nature spirits, guardian spirits, or "devas," from the Sanskrit word meaning "an order of **good** spirits." Hindu cosmology includes devas for each of the three kingdoms: animal, plant and mineral.

I once had the extraordinarily good fortune of seeing a cat deva in my grounds. When my cat, Buzzy, was at the brink of death, and I was filled with sorrow at the prospect of losing him, a semi-human form with cat-like features appeared in my grounds, holding a protective arm around Buzzy.

I didn't know whether it had come to take Buzzy to cat heaven or to offer protection in life, but whatever the eventual outcome of the illness, the message was clear: "Don't worry, your cat is protected." Miraculously, there was a full recovery. Animals too, have guardian angels.

TOTEM ANIMAL SPIRIT GUIDES

A totem is an object–usually a plant or animal–adopted by an individual, group or clan, as a sacred symbol. It serves as protector, guide, friend, teacher, etc.

According to Native American tradition, each of us has animal spirit guides ("totem" animals) which silently assist us in learning the lessons with which they are associated. For example:

If **Eagle** appears in the grounds as your totem animal, then you are being asked to learn how to live in the world of spirit while your feet are planted firmly on earth. Eagle teaches how to soar beyond the limits of 3-dimensional reality; to "see" from a higher perspective; and to overcome fear through faith in the "great spirit" in the sky.

If **Buffalo** appears to you, you are being asked to acknowledge the abundance in your life; to be thankful for all God's blessings.

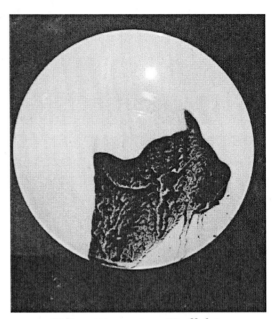

Bison (American Buffalo)

Cover illustration reprinted with permission from the artist, Dugald Stermer, and the publisher, Sasquatch Books, Seattle, WA.

Spirit Guide Face of "White Feather"
My client, of Native American descent, recognized her great grandmother, White Feather, from the feather's appearance just next to the face in the center circle.

33

RECOGNIZING TOTEM ANIMALS

How does the diviner distinguish between an animal appearing as a totem spirit guide or as an animal having some other meaning? My *personal experience* is that totem animals appear primarily in saucer grounds, while the same creature in a cup has the traditional interpretation. To be absolutely certain, provide all interpretations and let your subject choose.

Totem animals infrequently appear in the grounds, but when they do, bringing you their wisdom and teachings, know that you have been truly gifted by spirit.

LOVED ONES IN SPIRIT

Deceased loved ones rarely appear in cups, but, like angels, they occasionally come unbidden. On one occasion, however, a woman who believed she had been communicating with her deceased grandfather, requested his presence during a cup reading. A very short man wearing an old fashioned bowler hat appeared in her grounds, and was immediately recognized by the woman as her grandfather.

Although I *never* recommend making such a request, it apparently is possible—for some people at some time—to intentionally establish contact with loved ones in spirit.

PAST LIFE IMAGES

On occasion, images of past lives have been requested and received. One of my students received the image of a Roman warrior, clearly defined in the grounds, helmet and shield included.

Of course, there is no way to establish fact from fiction with regard to such images in a cup, unless they can be validated by past life regression or recorded documentation. If this is possible, then one more portal has been opened—a portal to the distant past—through the medium of coffee grounds.

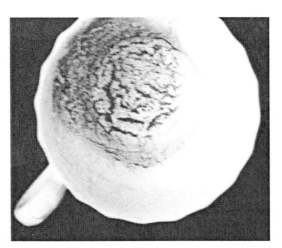

Face of Deceased Friend
Unknown to subject, a good friend passed away at about the time this face appeared in her grounds. She was informed of the death several weeks later.

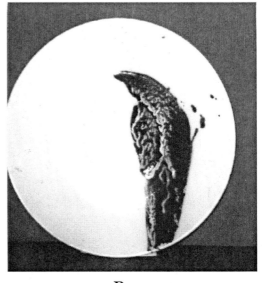

Raven
Sacred for its absent healing and spirit messages.

Devil
The dark figure sporting a tail (devil) seems to be doing battle with a small figure (angel?) Subject was contemplating a negative act.

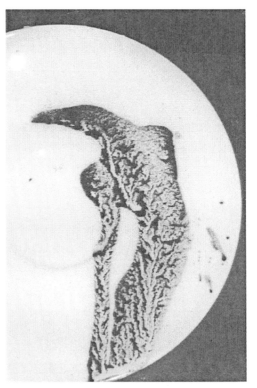

Man's Body, Vulture's Head
Warning of man with vulture-like mentality.

IN CONCLUSION

There appears to be no limit to the variety of miraculous images which appear in the grounds.

I have personally seen angels; spirit guides (both human and animal); deceased loved ones; mythological creatures such as unicorns, mermaids, dragons, centaurs, devils, and monsters, etc. I have also seen a fantastic giant sea creature, and too many other strange visions to recount.

These images do not appear frequently. Some were seen only once in a span of 35 years. When cup reading with coffee grounds, only one generalization consistently holds true: ***Expect the unexpected!***

TIMING EVENTS AND HOW TO PROCEED

TIMING EVENTS

THE PRESENT: The handle indicates the present, and is the dividing point between past and future.   All images seen in the grounds directly below and in a line with the handle, reflect the immediate present.

THE PAST: The past is measured in a *counter clockwise* direction away from the handle.   One-quarter of the distance around the cup is approximately three months past; one-half way around the cup–directly opposite the handle–is the six month position.

> Sometimes, *left-handed subjects* are read in reverse; the future is on the past side, and the past is on the future side.   It is essential that you validate this timing by consulting with the subject.

THE FUTURE: The future is measured in a *clockwise* direction away from the handle.   One-quarter of the distance around the cup is approximately three months into the future; one-half way around the cup–directly opposite the handle–is the six month position.

JUST BEYOND THE HANDLE: Images seen just slightly beyond the handle on the future side, refer to situations in the very near future; tomorrow, or within a few days.   The same principle applies to images seen just the other side of the handle, on the past side. They refer to yesterday, or the past few days.

It is difficult to be absolutely precise with regard to timing events, so it would be safe to say that images falling between the handle and the three month position on the future side, can most accurately be stated as: "Some time within the next three months."   On the past

The Handle
All images in line with the handle
indicate the immediate present.

The Past
3-month
position
(counter
clockwise
from the
handle).

The Future
3-month
position
(clockwise
from the
handle).

The Six-Month Position
Opposite the handle. Can represent
6 months past or 6 months into the
future.

THE BOTTOM OF THE CUP
Grounds at the bottom of the cup represent
the immediate present or very near future—
a few days at most.

LEFT-HANDED PEOPLE
Oftentimes (but not always), the cups of
left-handed subjects are read in reverse. The
past is read clockwise from the handle. You
need to verify events with subject's help.

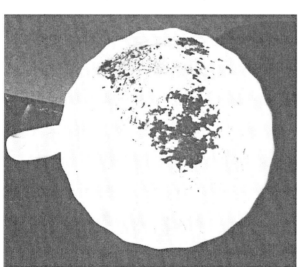

Ant (Hard Work)
Grounds at the bottom of the cup represent the immediate present or very near future (a few days at most). This image presaged a period of hard and concentrated effort.

Bird (Messenger)
The handle represents the immediate present. The encircled bird is beneath the handle, slightly to its left (the past). Subject received an important message the morning of her afternoon reading.

Rose (Token of Love)
This image appears about 3 ½ months into the future (clockwise from the handle). Love or romance coming?

side of the handle, "Some time within the past three months."

THE SIX MONTH POSITION—PAST OR FUTURE? Half-way around the cup in either direction, and directly opposite the handle, is the six month position. It can represent six months into the future, or six months past.

If, therefore, an image is there in the six month position, and you don't know whether it belongs to the past or future, describe what you see, offer an interpretation for the image, and allow your subject to determine whether it is past or future.

THE BOTTOM, THE THUMB-PRINT, THE SAUCER: Images found at the bottom of the cup; those left by the thumb being pressed into the grounds at the bottom of the cup; and those found in the saucer, all refer to the immediate present and/or very near future. Warning images, however (owl, bat, octopus, etc.), *always* refer to the immediate present.

Sometimes, saucers reveal images of "totem animals" which function as guides, helpers and teachers, according to Native American tradition. These images are not bound by conventional concepts of linear time. A totem animal guide can, for example, refer to a lesson needing your attention for as long as is necessary.

HOW TO PROCEED

THE SEQUENCE: There is a logical, step-by-step procedure for reading the grounds, which beginners find useful. It offers structure and method to a psychic art which, in fact, has no formal structure; no absolutes.

The following guidelines tell you where to start a reading and where to go from there. (Interpretation is not dealt with here; *see* Chapters 8 and 9 for interpretation Guidelines.)

FIRST, the Past: Start reading with the furthest image in the past. This has two advantages: (1) Past events may influence present or future circumstances; and (2) while predicted future events need follow-up for their validation, past events can be corroborated. Getting validation for your interpretation of a past situation builds a foundation of confidence in your accuracy.

SECOND, the Present: Move from the past toward the present in a clockwise direction, reading as you go. When you reach the images at the handle, you are looking at the immediate present.

Sometimes, grounds are seen only on one side of the handle. In that case, the only message of consequence is for that moment in time.

THIRD, the Future: Move into the future by reading in a clockwise direction away from the handle. Do not read past the six month position opposite the handle. While the psychic arts are not bound by ordinary clock time, few readers of coffee grounds divine beyond three to four months into the future.

FOURTH, the Bottom of the Cup: The grounds at the bottom of the cup refer to the immediate present or very near future. Read it after the rest of the cup has been read, and just prior to leaving a thumb-print. If the thumb-print is placed before the bottom of the cup is read, then whatever images are there will be irretrievably lost.

FIFTH, the Thumb-Print: The very last thing to be read within the cup itself is the thumb-print. If the grounds at the bottom are dark enough so that an impression can be left when a thumb is pressed into them, then the image which appears will reflect the last part of the reading, except for the saucer.

SIXTH, the Saucer: Saucer images do not usually appear to be related to the rest of the reading. Preferably, therefore, the saucer is read last, as if it were a separate little mini-reading.

MAKING A THUMB-PRINT

When a cup is turned upright for reading, there must be grounds at the bottom in order to make a thumb-print image. No grounds, no image.

1. Read the entire cup before leaving a thumb-print. The thumb-print is like the icing on a cake. It's not essential to a reading.

2. Slightly dampen the top joint of the thumb so that some of the dry or drying grounds will adhere to it when it is gently pressed into them.

3. Press the top joint of the thumb down into the grounds at the bottom of the cup and withdraw it without moving or twisting it. Press down, pick up.

4. If pressed too hard, only a white space will remain. However, if that white space has the distinct shape of something recognizable, interpret it as part of the reading.

5. If too little pressure is applied, none of the grounds will adhere to the thumb, and no discernable image will result.

6. If the correct amount of pressure is applied, only some of the grounds will adhere to the thumb, leaving a well-defined image in the bottom of the cup. Study it from all angles.

CONCLUSION

These guidelines suggest that you initially read from past to present to future, leaving the bottom of the cup, the thumb-print and saucer for last. Your preference may be to start with a prominent image and work around that, or to read in some other fashion. Eventually, your individual style will evolve.

MAKING A THUMB-PRINT

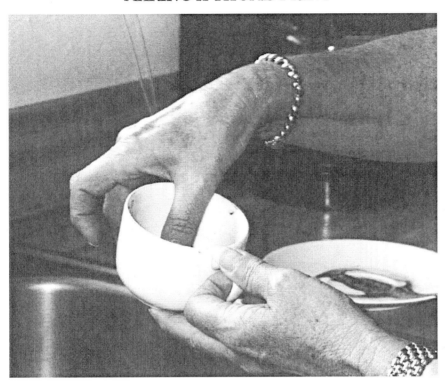

Thumb-Print Scotty Dog
(A faithful friend)
Thumb-print images represent
the immediate present or very
near future.

Chapter 8

INTERPRETING THE IMAGES, PART I

FIND THE MEANING

The fastest way to find the meaning of an image is to look it up in *Section II, The Symbols*. If an image has consistently recurred throughout history–in dreams, mythology, folk tales, etc.–then it is part of that universal memory bank known as *The Collective Unconscious.* and will most likely be listed in Section II, or in a book of symbols. If not, discuss the image with your subject, for whom it might have personal significance.

LITERAL OR SYMBOLIC

Images may be interpreted literally or symbolically. "A rose is a rose is a rose . . ." Or is it? The rose you see in the grounds may be the rose cut that morning to decorate your subject's table (literal interpretation), or it might represent the concept of love (symbolic interpretation).

PERSONAL SYMBOLS

While most images retain their traditional interpretations, others have meaning only for particular people.

A motorcycle with a rider always appeared in Jane's grounds preceding a visit from her South American friend, whose business involved the importation and distribution of motorcycles. While a horse with a rider symbolizes "a lover hurrying to you," in Jane's cup, a motorcycle with a rider carried the same message.

A white elephant traditionally refers to something which devours your finances, such as a house or car needing constant repair (unless the trunk is up, in which case it means "good luck"). For Dina, however, a white elephant always foretold a visit from her friend from Thailand, where white elephants are held sacred.

You can quickly distinguish between universally appearing symbols and personal symbols by simply asking your subject if an image has personal meaning.

DETAILS ARE IMPORTANT

The details of an image shed light upon its meaning. A hat means "honors bestowed," a dog (friend) wearing a hat means "honors bestowed upon a friend." A nearby initial or other sign might identify the specific friend.

A fish usually means "money coming," but if that fish has an open mouth, sharp teeth and a hungry look, then the meaning is reversed; money is being eaten up, money is *going out.*

SIZE OF THE IMAGE

The relative size of an image in the grounds reflects its relative importance. A big fish portends more money than a small one. A large face or figure is much more significant than a small one.

CONNECTED IMAGES

Images are sometimes physically connected, touching one another. Two images may also be connected by a line, or by a third image between them which touches both. When images are physically connected, they are usually interpreted as part of the same situation or event.

COMBINED IMAGES

A combined image contains two or more separate pictures in one image. For example, looking at an image from one direction, it appears to be a man's face in profile. From another direction, it appears to be a toad (a false flatterer). Combining the interpretation for each, the message becomes "A man who is a false flatterer."

Elephant's Head (left)
The usual meaning for an elephant, if the trunk is up, is "good luck." If down, it changes to "disappointment," or "bad luck."

Stylized Pig (below)
Turning the entire picture to its side, the thumb-print image of a pig appears. A pig means "good luck but danger of overindulgence."

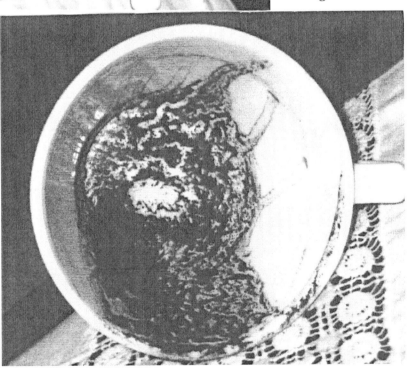

Combining the Images for a Final Interpretation
Taken together, these images constitute an admonition: Overindulgence (pig) will bring disappointment or bad luck (elephant trunk facing down). Subject has ulcerative colitis, an illness requiring strict dietary care. Super indulgence on a holiday weekend resulted in a serious flare of the illness.

My own cup periodically repeats the very comical combined image of a plump animal's body with a pig's face on one end and a hippopotamus' face on the other end. This a warning to me about my weight and tendency to overindulge a voraciously stubborn sweet tooth. My very humorous spirit guide is conscientiously reminding me that if I don't stop "pigging out," I'm going to look like a hippo!

Spirit Guides have various functions. Some just look after your health, safety and well being; others might assist with artistic, literary, or other creative endeavors, stimulating fresh ideas and inspiration. Whatever your guides do for you, a sense of humor and a good laugh are not precluded.

CHANGE PERSPECTIVE
Viewing images from different perspectives can reveal previously unnoticed configurations. After examining a cup in its upright position, tilt it, turn it around and turn it upside down. Examine the grounds again from different angles. Sometimes, leaving the cup alone for a period of time–perhaps a half-hour or more–can also change your vision of what it contains.

Chapter 9

INTERPRETING THE IMAGES, PART II

IMAGES WITH MULTIPLE INTERPRETATIONS

Many images have multiple meanings. For example, a bat's image has three possible interpretations, all of which are closely related: A worthless journey; a fruitless task; a warning. A fourth interpretation, however, might be describing something which needs to be done: "Give up everything which no longer serves your growth, emotional as well as material. You are about to experience a totally new beginning."

When an image has multiple meanings, present them all. Given a variety of options, subjects always recognize the one most valid for themselves.

THE BOTTOM OF THE CUP

Because grounds tend to accumulate at the bottom of the cup, clear images are not always found there. When they are, they usually carry a message for the immediate present or very near future (within a few days). However, some images may reflect something which is "beyond time," such as a spirit guide, a departed loved one, or a past life experience.

THUMB-PRINT IMAGES

The thumb-print image in the grounds at the bottom of the cup frequently carries a message of some significance for the immediate present or very near future. When I had a period of very concentrated work ahead of me, my thumb-print left the image of an ant, symbolizing activity, diligence, and hard work.

ANIMAL THUMB-PRINT IMAGES

These images sometimes relate to a subject's state of mind or being, or to an emotional, physical or psychological need. A dragonfly, for example, can symbolize a subject's need to look beyond the illusory shackles that bind him, a need to "follow his bliss."

THE SAUCER

While the origin of saucer-reading is unknown, it provides a useful complement to a cup reading. A young man who had just completed his ministerial studies and was about to be ordained, had the most exquisite and clearly defined image of a mountain lion in his saucer grounds.

If the image was a totem animal, then the message was related to the lesson of the mountain lion regarding the requirements of leadership; its responsibilities and rewards. In his new profession, this young man had to learn the specific lessons associated with mountain lion.

If, however, he was about to go hiking in the mountains of California, where mountain lion attacks have been known to occur, the message might be very different.

PUTTING IT ALL TOGETHER

THE HIDDEN MESSAGE: Some cups contain just a few, clear-cut images, and their messages are easily understood. Others have many scattered, seemingly unrelated or unrecognizable images which may, in fact, be accurately reflecting a hidden message, such as a subject's unfocused state of mind. Such a message may be profound, or may be reflecting nothing more than a temporary, inconsequential state of affairs.

IS THERE A THEME? In many cups, separate images refer to separate events or situations. Sometimes, however, numerous images are clearly related to each other, and signify an ongoing story or situation, or refer to a single event, the theme behind the pictures.

A student of mine was about to make a pilgrimage to India. His grounds held images of long and short journeys; an elephant with its trunk down (disappointment); temples; warning signs of illness (crosses); and a bat (a worthless journey). With confirmation from an astrologer, the young man chose to postpone the journey, but two companions who went contracted malaria and were forced to return home.

Another cup's happier theme related to a joyful union; a ring, a bouquet; a celebration feast; wedding bells; a marriage.

Bird at Rest
Good news message coming.

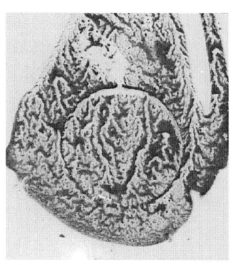

Horse's Head
(in center circle)
A lover.

Combined Image
Body of Great Dane (a good and faithful friend) with a lion's head (someone in a position of authority who will assist the subject). This image appeared a few days prior to a "healing" provided by a well-known healer who later became a friend.

51

Chapter 10

FINAL WORDS

Throughout these pages, guidelines have been presented for developing your skill as a psychic using coffee grounds to divine. Only four guidelines, however, are essential prerequisites to the success of anyone seriously involved in the business of divination.

1. IT ISN'T CAST IN STONE
Of the situations and events seen in the grounds, many will materialize, but others won't. Why?

A few, such as the timely passing of an elderly grandparent, are "fated" events over which we have no control. Others are the result of a series of circumstances which have led to the consequences foretold by the grounds.

There are, however, images which signify *potential* happenings. Imagine a road with a fork in it. Take the turn to the left, and a particular destination awaits you. Take the turn to the right, and a different outcome awaits you. In such a situation, what you see in the grounds is a *probable* outcome—one which has already been set in motion—but which can be changed by changing direction, even at the zero hour. A trip can be cancelled; a confrontation avoided.

It is important that your subject understand this, especially where warnings are concerned. Heeding a timely piece of advice can prevent a negative outcome, so what you see is not necessarily cast in stone.

2. THE TRUTH
There are many fine psychics who, like everyone else, have their "off days." A small percentage of them feel compelled to provide client satisfaction even when they have no messages to convey. They unwittingly tarnish the reputation of the psychic arts.

If you can't read on a given day, or can't read a particular cup, say so; set an appointment for another time. If you don't understand a pattern in the grounds, say so. Don't play guessing games; just describe what you see and elicit the subject's input. Guessing will demean your credibility.

When a suggestion is planted in a suggestible person's mind, the possibility exists that the prediction will be carried out through subconscious belief and behavior. This is what is known as a "self-fulfilling prophesy." This principle applies to positive as well as negative suggestions. An entire industry has sprung up around this concept: "Develop your self-esteem"; "Stop smoking"; "Lose weight"; "Heal yourself"; etc. etc. etc.

The point is that words are powerful tools of communication; so powerful that they can change the course of history. One book, the Bible, has changed western civilization forever; one speech can move a nation to war.

3. SPEAK WISELY

By wisely weighing your words, you can utilize their power to serve your subject's best interests. Communicate in a positive, constructive manner, with tact and diplomacy.

This does **not** mean that you cannot communicate a sorrowful message. If the message is in the grounds, it is meant to be understood and conveyed. Here, for example, is an unhappy message expressed positively:

> Your grandfather is approaching a time of freedom from
> pain and care, a time of significant spiritual transformation.

The power of words can make the difference between upliftment and despair; between a comforting or frightening reading.

4. OBSERVE YOURSELF COMMUNICATING

Facial expressions, tone of voice and body language are unconscious forms of communication. Become aware of your unconscious language. Are you knitting your brows? Speaking excitedly, or in a calm and reassuring manner? Do you reveal a negative emotional reaction when peering into a cup? Practice being aware.

THE ROLE OF THE DIVINER

People consult psychics for a number of reasons. Many want to know about a particular life situation, or just wish to satisfy a general curiosity. Others, in unhappy circumstances, seek advice, comfort and/or encouragement. Some are in search of their mission in life–their path, or destiny–best defined by numerology or astrology. There are any number of reasons why psychics are consulted.

Still, the role of the psychic, or diviner, has not been defined. Is the psychic a messenger-seer, counselor, or more? The kind and quality of reading one receives will reflect the personality and capability of the reader.

THE IDEAL READING

The ideal reading will be helpful and encouraging, even when sorrowful events are seen. Each cup must be handled according to its special contents, and the personality of the subject taken into account. Quick, intuitive judgments are frequently called for by a reader. If the four guidelines outlined above are consistently applied, an ideal reading is more likely to result.

CONCLUSION

Several of the world's great spiritual traditions give little credit to psychic ability; the desired goal is spiritual growth resulting from disciplined practice and selfless service. Nevertheless, there are as many paths to spiritual awareness as those who tread them.

Everything starts somewhere, and if the art of reading coffee grounds is used for the purpose of helping others, it becomes one of those paths.

Knowing that the practice of divination can alter the course of a life, I trust that those who were meant to explore these pages will discover and use them wisely.

SECTION II

THE SYMBOLS

Chapters 11 through 16

PART 1 - THE HUMAN FAMILY

INTRODUCTION

People may be interpreted literally, referring to specific individuals, or figuratively. For example, a fetus in the grounds may represent an actual pregnancy (literal interpretation), or it could refer to a new idea or project (figurative interpretation).

A costumed figure can represent an actual person wearing a costume, or it can represent a location, an historical era, a past life, a spirit guide, or something else. For example, the grounds of a naval officer about to be shipped overseas to an unknown destination showed a male figure wearing a long white caftan and fez in a desert environment (a fez is a brimless felt hat characteristic of Muslim dress in the Middle East). This type of clothing symbolized a location; a Middle Eastern destination for my client.

Another example of a costumed figure representing something other than a real person was the image of a black-robed woman wearing a veil. My client had just landed a role in the operetta "The Merry Widow." I, as the reader, could never have interpreted the true meaning of this image. All I could do was describe what I saw, a "widow in black," and allow the subject to fill in the rest. Taking such an approach alleviates the need for guesswork on the part of the reader, and encourages an environment in which client and diviner can freely interact.

Initials, astrological symbols, numbers, etc., may reveal a specific person's identity. Examine nearby images for the clues which identify a face or figure in the grounds.

Acrobat   Balance.

Arm   Help, protection, justice.

Baby   A new addition to the family.
                           A literal baby (look for identifying marks).
                           The birth of a new project or idea.

Beard   Masculinity, bravery.

Bones   A health warning.

Breasts   Motherhood, nurturance, fertility, abundance.

Bride   A forthcoming marriage.

Buddha   Buddhist practice.
                           Enlightenment, healing, wholeness.

Child   Innocence, spontaneity.
                           An unexpected expense.
                           A specific child (look for identifying marks).

Clown   Pleasure, gayety.
                           Irreverence, mockery.
                           Danger of deception.

Crone   Prophesy, old age.

Ear   Listen to your intuition
                           Others may be listening to and evaluating your words.

Eye   Observation, watchfulness.
                           Inspect all proposals carefully.
                           Be wary, you are being watched.

Feet   If bare, humbleness.
                           Poverty.
                           A pilgrimage.

Fetus   Gestation of a new idea or project.
                           Pregnancy.

Finger	Pointing the way.
Hand	If open, generosity of spirit. Help, protection, authority, a blessing. If closed, secrecy, or miserliness.
Infant	See "baby."
Jockey	Speculation.
Man	A visitor is coming. A specific man (look for identifying marks). If in costume, he can represent a location, an historical era, a past life experience, or a spirit guide.
Monk	Spiritual matters at hand. A time for retreat and contemplation.
Nun	Commitment to God, service, or repentance.
Nurse	Sickness, services will be called upon.
Priest	Inner wisdom. Externally imposed prohibitions.
Rider	News arriving quickly. If on a horse, a visit from a lover.
Runner	Message(s) coming.
Skeleton	A death.
Skull	A literal death or the symbolic death of a project or idea.
Teeth	Aggression, insincerity. Fear of aging.
Thumb	Power, control.
Twins	Duality, or someone born in the sign of Gemini.
Woman	Usually, a specific woman. Look for identifying marks. If in costume, she can signify a location, an historical era, a past life experience, a spirit guide, etc.

Chapter 11

PART 2

MYTHOLOGICAL BEINGS AND OTHER FANTASTIC CREATURES

Angel   Spiritual help and divine protection.

Anubis   Jackal-headed Egyptian god of the underworld.
                     Judgment is at hand.

Basilisk   A mythological creature resembling a winged lizard
                     which kills with its breath or gaze. A ***warning*** of
                         extreme danger, even death.

Centaur   Body of a horse with torso and head of a man - symbol
                         of Sagittarius.
                     Healer, teacher, renegade, knowledge bearer and seeker
                         of higher truths.
                     You must overcome your physical passions in order to
                         evolve mentally and spiritually.

Cupid   Romanticism, erotic love, a lover on the horizon.

Devil   Temptation, greed, false values, evil, sin.

Dragon   A sudden and dramatic change.
                     Upheaval, problems, a need to overcome fear.
                     Can refer to an Asian location.

Fairy   Fun, youth, a season of romance.

Giant   Brutish and untamed animal instincts. ***Warning.***

Gnome   A hidden treasure.

Gorgon   Any of the three sisters of Greek mythology (including
                         Medusa) whose hair was comprised of writhing
                         snakes.
                     A terrifying, horrible, dangerous woman.

Griffin

A creature with the head and wings of an eagle and the body of a lion. Extreme danger of bodily harm. A severe *warning.*

Harpy

A creature with the body of a vulture and the head of a woman.
The most destructive aspects of women.
An agent of sudden death. *Warning.*

Hydra

The nine-headed serpent slain by Hercules. Each head was replaced by two when cut off. Symbolizes a persistent evil which keeps arising and is difficult to subdue. *Warning.*
Symbolic of the challenges encountered on the spiritual path.

Mars

God of war, ruler of Aries.
Aggression, desire, male sexuality.

Medusa

Her hair of writhing snakes was so terrifying that looking at her turned one to stone.
An extremely dangerous and cunning woman. *Warning.*

Mermaid

Temptation and seduction. A luring away from one's goals and purpose. *Warning.*

Monster

Evil and destruction, plotting, a dark force. *Warning.*

Neptune

Roman god of the seas and ruler of Pisces.
Spiritual strength, escapist tendencies, artistic talent, photography and the dance.
Floods, rain, caution if traveling by water.

Ouroboros

Circular image of a snake with its tail in its mouth.
Symbolizes the cycle of eternal life.

Pegasus

The winged horse. Symbolizes poetic inspiration.

Phoenix   Mythical fire bird which immolates itself every 100 years
                       and rises again from its own ashes. Symbol of immor-
                       tality and reincarnation.

Pluto   Lord of the underworld. Death to old conditions,
                       transformation and regeneration.

Sirens   Sea creatures with the heads and breasts of women and
                       the bodies of fish. Their irresistible song lured
                       unwary sailors to their deaths. Odysseus plugged the
                       ears of his crew with wax in order to escape them.
                       A fatally alluring lover.
                       Danger by water. ***Warning.***

Unicorn   Purity, chastity, gentleness, truth.
                       Sexuality tamed by spiritual love.

Venus   Goddess of love, associated with Taurus and Libra.
                       Romance, female sexuality, creativity.
                       Comfort and luxury.
                       A lover.

Chapter 12

ANIMALS, INSECTS, REPTILES AND SEA LIFE

INTRODUCTION

Literal or Figurative: Like human faces and figures, animal images can be interpreted literally or figuratively.

The appearance of household pets in the grounds is a common occurrence. These are interpreted literally; that spaniel you see is Ginger, your subject's dog (literal interpretation). If not a real, specific animal, then a dog symbolizes "a good and faithful friend" (figurative interpretation).

Multiple Interpretations: Many animals can be interpreted in more than one way. If next to the animal listed in its proper alphabetical order you find more than one interpretation, then if in doubt about which interpretation to select, present them all. Your subject will know the one that best applies.

Unlisted Animals: Our tendency to anthropomorphize animals (project human traits upon them), is what gives rise to many of the interpretations found here.

If, therefore, you perceive an animal in the grounds for which there is no listed meaning, reverse the process. What are its primary traits and habits? What is its habitat? Assume that the creature symbolizes a person with similar traits and habits, or that the creature refers to a specific location. A panda, for example, could represent a very bear-like and cuddly person, or it could refer to China.

Again, cup-reading is an art; nothing is immutable. So stretch your psychic faculties and just enjoy the process.

Alligator   A thick-skinned, insensitive person.
                       Possible treachery lying in wait.

Ant(s)   Activity, diligence, and hard work ahead.

Anteater   Bad luck.

Ape   Deception in love.
                       Sin, malice, cunning, lust.

Armadillo   America's Southwest.
                       Learn to say *no* to impositions placed upon your personal
                           space and time. Be tactful but firm.

Bat   A worthless journey, a fruitless task. ***Warning.***
                       Give up everything which no longer serves your growth.
                           A totally new beginning awaits you.

Bear   A bitter quarrel, especially if there are two bears. Avoid
                           actions which may elicit hostile behavior from others.
                       Time out for healing, meditation, introspection, and the
                           utilization of your intuitive faculties.

Beaver   A builder, architect, or someone in the construction
                           trades.
                       A house or home in the works; home improvement.

Bee(s)   Activity, industry, sagacity, organization. A busy time
                           ahead.

Beetle   Scandal.
                       In ancient Egypt, the scarab symbolized rebirth. You
                           may experience a new birth arising out of the decay
                           of the old.

Boar   A loud-mouthed, boorish person.
                       If white, spiritual attainment.
                       If black, power perverted. Evil.

Buffalo   Abundance.
                       True abundance results from prayer and thankfulness
                           for all God's blessings.

Bull
Someone born in the sign of Taurus.
A country where there are bullfights.
Male strength, machismo, creative energy.
You must learn to develop ***temperance*** and tame the ego.

Butterfly
Frivolity and innocent pleasure.
The life cycle of the butterfly is a lesson in metamorphosis. Know when to let go of the old and embrace the new.

Camel
A burden to be patiently borne. Temperance, endurance, strength and moderation are required.
The Middle East, North Africa, or other places where camels are found.

Cat
A household pet.
An insincere friend.
Nature's wisdom and mystery.

Caterpillar
(Also larvae). Metamorphosis.
Greed and ugliness.

Cockroach
Filth, vermin, a low form of life.
An infestation.

Cow
A female born in the sign of Taurus.
Dignity, strength, passive endurance.
Comforts at home if on or facing the cup's handle.

Coyote
Beware a trickster.
Avoid nefarious schemes or sales pitches.

Crab
Someone born in the sign of Cancer.
A secret enemy. ***Warning.***

Crocodile
Treachery, greed, hypocrisy. ***Warning.***

Deer
With antlers, a message or visit from the North.
Without antlers, a need for unconditional love, caring, gentleness and nurturing.

Dinosaur   Extreme anger, raw primitive emotions.
                                Caution is advised, avoid confrontation. ***Warning.***

Dog   A good and faithful friend.
                                A household pet.

Dolphin   A light bearer. You are meant to teach and inspire.
                                Divination, wisdom, and the power of regeneration.
                                Replenish your vitality through meditation and breath-
                                        ing exercises.

Donkey   Patience, contentment, endurance. Patience and
                                        perseverance will overcome obstacles.

Dragonfly   You must throw off the illusionary shackles which bind
                                        you and "follow your bliss."

Eel   Someone slimy and "slippery as an eel."
                                Danger, a sudden attack. ***Warning.***

Elephant   With trunk up, good luck. Trunk down, disappointment.
                                If white with trunk down, then burdensome expenses
                                        from something needing constant repair.
                                A sacred animal in Thailand; royalty.

Elk   A message or visit to or from the North.
                                Sensible pacing and a healthy life style can strengthen
                                        your stamina and help you reach your goals.

Ermine   A symbol of purity because of the whiteness of its fur.

Fish   Money coming. The bigger the fish, the larger the sum.
                                        If, however, the fish has an open mouth and hungry
                                        look, money will go out, be eaten up.
                                Two fish swimming in opposite directions--someone
                                        born in the sign of Pisces.

Fly   Vexations. Bringer of disease.

Fox   Someone "foxy," someone playing tricks. Avoid quest-
                                        ionable sales pitches and nefarious schemes.

Frog   Servility. A false flatter. ***Warning.***

Giraffe   Treachery afoot. ***Warning.***

Goat   Someone born in the sign of Capricorn.
                                Infidelity.

Grasshopper   A plague is coming.

Hippopotamus   A strong rebuke against overindulgence.

Horse   A horse's head, a lover. If galloping with a rider,
                                    a visit or message from a lover. If surrounded
                                    by thick grounds and wavy lines, delays.

Jackal   Cowardice, misfortune.

Kangaroo   Anything Australian, including messages to or
                                    from Australia.

Koala Bear   See "Kangaroo."

Ladybug   Good luck.

Lamb   A young person born in the sign of Aries.
                                Fortunate changes in the Spring.
                                If surrounded by thick grounds, danger of letting youth
                                    slip away in trivial pursuits.

Leopard   A warrior, a hunter.
                                 Proud, strong, courageous, royalty.

Lion   Someone born in the sign of Leo.
                                Strength, courage, majesty, fortitude.
                                A powerful person who will assist the subject.

Lizard   The American Southwest.
                                Are you manifesting your thoughts and dreams? Why?

Monkey   Deception in love.
                                Mischief making, intrusive inquisitiveness.

Moose

A message or visit from (or to) the North.
Take pride in your achievements, but don't confuse self-respect with egotism. Value the accomplishments of others as well as your own.

Mountain Lion

Leadership, strength, courage, responsibility.
Dignity and honor, rather than authoritarian inflexibility, are the keys to successful leadership.

Mouse

Danger of theft. ***Warning.***
Avoid poverty through neglected opportunities.
Tidy and organized, you may lose sight of the forest for the trees. Develop a broader perspective.

Octopus

Plots, a danger signal. ***Warning.***

Otter

Life has become too serious. Discard your worries and fears and return to spontaneity and joy.

Ox

Creative energy, power, patience and strength.
Those who silently bear their yoke while laboring for the benefit of others.

Penguin

See "Birds."

Pig

Good luck, but danger of overindulgence. Self-control is called for. ***Caution.***

Porcupine

You need a break from the responsibilities of adulthood. Make time to have fun, to be silly and childish.

Rabbit

A friend in trouble needs your help.
Give up irrational fears and worries–they add nothing to your span of life.

Ram

Someone born in the sign of Aries.
Strength, virility, procreative power.

Rat

Deception, treachery, loss through enemies. ***Warning.***

Reindeer

A message or visit from (or to) the North.
A Christmas celebration or vacation.

Rhinoceros	A large, solitary person. Generally good natured, but subject to unpredictable bursts of aggression. ***Caution advised***.
Salamander	If surrounded by flames, a symbol of the good soul who passes through the fires of temptation unharmed.
Scorpion.	The least evolved manifestation of the sign of Scorpio. Higher manifestations are the eagle and the phoenix. Treachery, jealousy, evil, destruction. ***Warning.***
Seahorse	Because the male seahorse carries its newborn in its pouch, it has become a male homosexual symbol.
Shark	A ***warning*** of extreme danger, even death. Greed, theft, scheming and plots.
Skunk	A really rotten person. Your physical bearing reflects your self-perception. Walk tall and straight, project self-respect.
Snail	Sluggishness. An admonition to speed up.
Snake	Enmity, deception, treachery, falsehood. Time to shed your old skin and move on into the new life which awaits you.
Spider	Cunning, secrecy, treachery, subterfuge. ***Warning.*** Danger of getting caught in an entangling situation.
Squirrel	Know the difference between hoarding and planning for the future. To prepare for times of change, get rid of unnecessary baggage.
Starfish	Enduring love. Love conquers all.
Swordfish	Danger, a ***warning.***
Tiger	Someone fierce, courageous and magnificent. India and the Malay Peninsula to Siberia.
Toad	Servility. A false flatterer. ***Warning.***

Turtle

Triumph after difficulties. If surrounded by thick, dark grounds, problems will resolve with persevering effort.

Whale

A major expense.
Presages a time of darkness followed by new beginnings, a rebirth.

Wolf

Intrigues, greed, theft and swindling.
A lustful man, a "wolf."
To Native Americans, Wolf symbolizes the teacher and pathfinder. Teach and share your knowledge.

Worms

Shame and disgrace.
An infestation.

Zebra

A call to foreign lands, adventures overseas.
A foreign lover.
A secret affair.

BIRDS

INTRODUCTION

In general, birds are interpreted as messengers.   Specific birds, however, have more specific meanings. The birds listed in this chapter all have specific meanings.

Some other generalizations are as follows:

Birds at rest::   A fortunate message; a stroke of good luck.

A flock of birds: A gathering.
A change of circumstances

Flying Birds: Messages coming quickly.
In rare circumstances, flying birds can symbolize
    a journey of release, renunciation and
    atonement.

A Bird's Nest: A secure family home.
Affection within the family.

Blackbird

Symbol of death.
Temptations of the flesh, sin.

Canary

A lover.
A beautiful voice.

Chicken

A project successfully completed.

Crane

Maternal love and nurturance.
Vigilance and protection.
Loyalty and an upstanding life.
Enlightenment for the spiritual seeker.

Crow

A bird of ill omen. In Northern Europe, a symbol of the
    death goddess, Valkyries.
A knowledge of the mysteries.
Beyond the temporal mores of your culture lie the
    eternal truths of God's law. You must live by these
    eternal truths.

Cuckoo

A messenger of spring.
A good omen.

Dove

Peace, innocense, purity.
A messenger of love.
Two doves--marital love and fidelity.

Duck

Good news from a distance, from "over the water."
Financial gain in business.

Eagle

Spiritual enlightenment, worldly power, royalty.
A baby eagle refers to a beginner on " the path."
It is time now to soar above your limitations and follow
    your soul's true calling.
A spiritual retreat is advised.

Falcon

Swiftness and strength, a hunter, royalty.
Your spirit has the power to heal or destroy; the choice
    is yours. Avoid evil thoughts and actions and direct
    your power to the benefit of others.

Goose

Watchfulness, foresight, love, good news.
A symbol of God's love for all earth's creatures.

Hawk

A divine messenger. Note the omens and signs around you. Counsel others when you are spiritually and psychologically ready. "Healer, heal thyself . . . "

Hen

Maternal care, protection of young.
A project well completed.

Hummingbird

Joy and a renewed awareness of life's beauty are imminent.
An urgent summons from a friend.

Lark

The humbleness of priesthood.

Ostrich

Hiding from the truth by burying one's head in the ground.

Owl

Wisdom and prophesy.
Bad luck, failure, danger.
Owl actually protects us by forewarning of ominous events. Thus, he is frequently perceived as a "bird of ill omen."

Parrot

Mockery, malicious gossip.
Mischief brewing, scandal.

Peacock

Worldly pride, vanity and ostentation.
Too much emphasis on external appearances.

Pelican

Parental devotion.
Self-sacrifice for one's children.

Penguin

An invitation to a formal affair.

Pigeon

Symbol of love.

Quail

Good luck.
The coming of spring.

Raven

The gift of magic and long-distance healing.
Messenger of war, sickness or death (bird of ill omen).
Trouble through thoughtless conversation.

Chapter 13   *Birds*

Rooster

Vanity, a braggart.
One who struts with self-importance.

Sparrow

Christian symbol of the lowly and humble who are,
   nevertheless, beloved and protected by God.

Stork

A baby is on its way.
Spring is coming.
Good luck.

Swallow

Because of the regularity of its yearly migration, it is
   a Christian symbol of resurrection.

Swan

A new love interest.
Psychic ability must be acknowledged and worked with.

Turkey

A Thanksgiving celebration.
You must learn to give without expectation of return.
A bomb, a bummer, a "real turkey." (Slang)

Vulture

Cruelty, theft, greed, oppression.

Chapter 14

THE PLANT WORLD
Flowers, Fruits, Trees, etc.

Acorn	Prosperity.
Almond	Fertility. Divine favor.
Almond tree	Sign of spring.
Apple	Love, desire, temptation, fruitfulness.
Apple blossoms	Wedding flowers.
Apple tree	A change for the better.
Bamboo	Friendship, good luck.
Banana tree	Transience.
Beech tree	Divination, endurance, prosperity.
Carnation	Symbol of love.
Cedar tree	Immortality.
Clover	Symbol of Ireland. Four-leaf clover, good luck.
Cherry	Sweetness of character.
Corn	Abundance
Cypress	Sacred tree of life. Longevity, immortality.
Daisy	Innocense. Happiness in the spring.
Daffodil	New hope.

Date Palm	God's blessings to the just.
Elm tree	Dignity
Ferns	Restlessness, change of desires. Humility and sincerity.
Fig tree	Abundance.
Fir tree	Spirituality, patience.
Forrest	A place of peace, refuge and meditation. A mysterious place where magical or significant events occur.
Fruit	Abundance, fortunate if in season. Refreshment, new life, fulfillment.
Garden	Promise of personal growth.
Garlic	Protection.
Gourd	The womb, fertility.
Grapes	Revelry. Love ambitions satisfied.
Grove	A sacred place.
Iris	Purity.
Ivy	Loyal friends and lasting affection.
Leaves	Happiness, success. A means of divination.
Lemon	Fidelity, purity, protection.
Lily	Purity.
Lily of the Valley	Return of spring. New beginnings in the spring.

76

Linden Tree	Healing properties. Joy, beauty, feminine attributes.
Lotus	A sacred flower of Hinduism and Buddhism. Female fertility. Purity, spiritual fulfillment.
Mushroom	Shelter. A woodland home.
Oak tree	Strength, faith, virtue, perseverance, bravery. Long life and good health.
Olive branch	Symbol of peace.
Olive tree	Good fortune.
Orange	A fertility symbol.
Palm tree	Nourishment, abundance, the "tree of life." May indicate a location with palm trees.
Peach	Virtuous mind and speech. Female sexual symbol.
Peach tree	Symbol of spring.
Pear	Love of humanity.
Pine tree	Longevity, fertility, endurance.
Plants	Plants symbolize the life cycle–birth, maturity, death and rebirth. Specific plants have specific meanings.
Pomegranate	Uterine fertility. The life cycle of birth, death and rebirth.
Reeds	Humility, sacrifice.

Rose	Love and beauty (if red).
	Virginal love, purity (if white).
Shamrock	See "Clover."
Strawberry	Righteousness.
	The fruit of good labor.
Sunflower	Nature at its fullest.
Thorns	Grief, tribulation, sorrow.
Trees	Generally, trees mean protection. Specific trees have specific meanings.
	Long life and good health if strong and healthy, but sickness or death if withered and dying.
Vine	Fruitfulness and long life.
	A protected place.
Violets	Modesty and sweetness.
Weeping Willow	Grace, beauty, strength.
	The coming of spring.
	Death and mourning.
Wheat	Nurturance.
Yew tree	Death, mourning, immortality.

Chapter 15

ASTROLOGICAL AND NUMEROLOGICAL SYMBOLS

THE ASTROLOGICAL SYMBOLS

INTRODUCTION

In coffee grounds, astrological symbols are sometimes perceived as identifying marks. If, for example, a male figure had the image of the sign of Aries on it or next to or touching it, then it would be interpreted as "a male born in the sign of Aries."

The same identification could be made from the image of a ram, the animal associated with the sign of Aries. Oftentimes, the animal associated with a particular sign will identify a person. Sometimes these are combined images. Recently, a client of mine had the combined image of a woman's body with a cow's head in her grounds. This image referred to her daughter, who was born in the sign of Taurus. A bull would have identified a male Taurus; a cow the female Taurus.

Astrological symbols appearing in the grounds might also carry messages. The symbol for the planet Neptune could forewarn a hurricane, or something else having to do with water. The symbol for the sign of Gemini might refer to the month of June, or to something having to do with twins.

Every symbol must be interpreted within the context of its surrounding images.

THE SIGNS

Aries "The Ram" ♈ Strong, self-directed, adventurous, pioneering, impulsive, overly direct.

Taurus "The Bull" ♉ Practical, artistic, lovers of beauty, patient, stubborn, self-indulgent.

Gemini "The Twins" ♊ Versatile, adaptable, restless, intelligent, inquisitive, inconsistent.

Cancer, "The Crab" ♋ Sensitive, instinctual, protective, affectionate, possessive, moody.

Leo "The Lion" ♌ Courageous, loyal, generous, enthusiastic, egotistical, arrogant.

Virgo "The Virgin" ♍ Patient, modest, orderly, analytical, cautious, perfectionistic.

Libra "The Scales" ♎ Conscientious, responsible, diplomatic, romantic, idealistic, represses anger.

Scorpio "The Scorpion, Eagle, or Phoenix" ♏ Imaginative, determined, powerful, reserved, secretive, resentful.

Sagittarious "The Archer" ♐ Freedom loving, adventurous, versatile, optimistic, capricious, blatantly honest.

Capricorn "The Goat" ♑ Strong, purposeful, practical, reliable, ambitious, self-serving.

Aquarius "The Water Bearer" ♒ Outgoing, individualistic, independent, inventive, fervent, dogmatic, detached.

Pisces "The Fish" ♓ Compassionate, serving, artistic, spiritual, intuitive, escapist.

THE PLANETS

The Sun	☉	Will, life force, power, creativity leadership, pride.
The Moon	☽	Subconscious mind, emotions, imagination, intuition, femininity, motherhood, habit patterns.
Mercury	☿	Intelligence, communication, adaptability, versatility, analysis, nervousness.
Venus	♀	Love, sensuality, art, creativity, luxury, self-indulgence.
Mars	♂	Energy, courage, self-will, passion, desire, combativeness.
Jupiter	♃	Expansion, abundance, religion, philosophy, extravagance, imperiousness.
Saturn	♄	Limitation, discipline, self-preservation, responsibility, conventionality, old age.
Uranus	♅	Freedom, originality, invention, independence, rebelliousness, detachment.
Neptune	♆	Idealism, spirituality, artistry, psychism, impracticality, escapism.
Pluto	♇	Transformation, decay, regeneration, healing, obsessions, destruction.

THE ASTEROIDS

Ceres	⚳	Mothers and nurturing; food, cooks and restaurants; agriculture and ecology; service occupations; helpfulness and caring; grief at human suffering; production; consumption and the market place.

THE ASTEROIDS (CONTINUED)

Pallas Wisdom and the thinking principle; justice and human rights; pattern perception and creation; self-determination; warrior woman in a man's world; the power of prophesy; weaving, crafts, and creations (children) of the mind, not body.

Juno Gracious and refined life style; decorating, entertaining, parties; marriage, childbirth; women, children and minorities; possessiveness and jealousy; powerlessness, seduction, the victim.

Vesta Home, hearth, sanctuary, protection; safety, security, safes, locks and keys; investments, stocks, bonds, etc.; vows, tradition, roots; nuns, priests, chastity, celibacy; focused concentration and total dedication to one's purpose.

THE NUMBERS

INTRODUCTION

Numbers occasionally appear in coffee grounds. They usually have significance only for the subject; a birthday, anniversary, or some other date to remember.

But unlike numbers as digits, numbers as symbols represent universal principles which have to do with creation and the unfolding and progression of life itself. These grand cosmic concepts eventually filter down to the level of humanity, and are then applied to mankind in more personal terms.

For example, cosmically, the Number One represents the Monad, the first indivisible principle, the unity from which all manifestation proceeds. As applied to human affairs, One is simply interpreted as "new beginnings," among other things.

Following are some key words associated with the numbers One through Nine and Eleven and Twenty-two (known as "Master Numbers" because they bestow special gifts and are extremely demanding).

As symbols for universal concepts applied to the human condition, numbers have a depth and breadth of meaning barely touched upon in the few key words used here to describe them.. **Numerology**, the **Science of Number as Symbol**, is a profound and complex lifetime study.

For the purpose of divining from coffee grounds, these limited descriptions will suffice.

83

ONE   Independence, self-reliance, initiative, innovation, leadership. New beginnings, activity, change.

TWO   Partnership, nurturing, a time-out period to nurture the seeds planted under the One. Parenthood, emotional intensity, diplomacy.

THREE   Creativity and self-expression. Communication, writing, love, romance, sociability. Development of talents and expanded social interaction.

FOUR   Hard work, organization, discipline. Slow moving, building foundations, limitation, patience and endurance.

FIVE   Freedom, adaptability, curiosity, versatility, movement, change, travel. A time for letting go of outworn patterns–people, places, things, etc.–and embracing the new.

SIX   Responsibility, domesticity, adjustment and service. Marriage, family matters and home conditions take precedence. Service to the intimate family and/or larger family, the community.

SEVEN   Perfection of mind and craft, subjective development, the perfected specialist. Spiritual or occult wisdom, philosophy, analysis, religion, seclusion, spiritual over material values.

EIGHT   Independence, efficiency, ambition. The right use and not abuse of power. Attainment, authority, business/money matters. Financial gain (or strain). Courage.

NINE   Tolerance, compassion, selfless service, high art, long distance travel , universality, a global outlook. Transformations (endings and new beginnings). Mastery, completion.

ELEVEN   Idealism, illumination, inspiration, Prophetic, visionary,
                             escapist. Creative and spiritual accomplishment;
                             nervous times.

TWENTY-TWO   Practical idealism, mastery, humanitarianism, power,
                             success. Accomplishment, hard work, expansion of
                             consciousness. Globalism, social service.

Chapter 16

EVERYTHING ELSE

Airplane		If moving skyward, a rise in status. If broken, an ominous omen. A trip by air.
Abbey		A place of retreat and protection.
Abyss		Impending danger. *Warning.* Physical or psychic death.
Altar		A holy sacrifice.
Anchor		Good luck, protection of journeys by water.
Ankh		An ancient Egyptian symbol of eternal life. The union of male and female principles.
Antlers		Male sexuality. A message from the North.
Apron		Work.
Arch		A gateway from one state of consciousness to another. Protection, purification, a happy marriage, a fresh start.
Arrow		Bad news.
Avalanche		Impending disaster. *Warning.*
Awning		Protection.
Axe		Authority, power, justice. Punishment and judgment. The double-headed axe (labrys) is a lesbian symbol found in jewelry, art, etc.
Ball and Chain		Onerous responsibilities.

Banner	A rallying call.
Banquet	A festive occasion.
Barrel	If whole, good luck. If broken, changing circumstances.
Basket	Abundance, a gift. An addition to the family.
Bath	Cleansing and regeneration.
Bell	A call to prayer. Recognition, success, a possible marriage.
Blindfold	Blindness.
Boat	An unexpected journey with secrets revealed. A transition.
Book	If open, something easy to understand. If closed, something secretive or mysterious.
Boot	Removal, the "kickout." ***Caution.***
Bottle	Sacred knowledge.
Bouquet	Festivities. Completion of desires.
Box	The unconscious. A precious secret.
Branch	Victory.
Bread	Nourishment, physical or spiritual.
Bridge	A favorable journey and outcome. A crossing over, a transition.
Broomstick	Time for a change, a "clean sweep." A witch or witch-like person is nearby.

Caduceus	A staff entwined by two snakes, symbol of the medical profession, of healing and healers.
Cage	Restrictions, self-imposed or otherwise. A cry for liberation.
Cake	A special occasion, a ceremony.
Candle	Protection, enlightenment.
Castle	Unexpected luck, an historic place, protection, refuge. Hopes fulfilled, spiritual attainment. If black, then failure and disappointment.
Cauldron	A magical vessel which confers abundance, knowledge, strength, healing, enlightenment, inspiration, nourishment, regeneration and rebirth.
Cave	Earth's womb. A symbolic place of birth, death, and regeneration.
Celtic Cross	Contains a circular band around the cross. Symbolizes the sun and eternity.
Chains	Restraints, restrained sexuality, an unconscious repression.
Chair	An unexpected visitor. Authority.
Chalice	Immortality.
Chariot	Become the driver, the master of your destiny.
Chimney	A link between heaven and earth, between psychics and spirits.
Circles	Completion, wholeness, perfection.
Cliff	The end of the road. A decision is called for.
Clock	Time is running out. ***Warning.***

Clouds	Problems, obstacles, delays.
Club	Brute force. ***Warning.***
Coffin	A tedious illness, death.
Comet	A sudden unexpected event. A change of circumstances.
Compass	Travel. A need for fresh bearings.
Convent	Dedication to divine service, restrictions, sacrifices.
Cornucopia	Prosperity, abundance.
Crescent Moon	New beginning, new life.
Cross	Sickness, suffering. Cross within a circle–forced restraint.
Crown	Success and honors.
Crutch	Physical deformity. Assistance, support.
Crystal	Wisdom and hidden power.
Cube	Stability.
Cup	Love and happiness.
Dagger	Aggression, anger. ***Warning.*** Avoid hasty decisions.
Dashes	Projects in the works, enterprises afoot.
Diamond	An engagement or marriage gift.
Dots	Money.
Drum	Quarrels, war, disturbances.

Easel	Support, success, an artist.
Egg	Increase, luck. Birth of a new project or idea. The source of life, hope, resurrection.
Fan	Flirtation, an invitation.
Feather	Freedom of flight, ascension, divination.
Fire	Danger, purification, a passion.
Flotilla	Business success, new projects.
Flying Carpet	Shamanic initiation preparatory to enlightenment.
Fog	A mystery, something secret or mystical. Confusion of the soul before attaining enlightenment. Confusion, inability to see clearly.
Fountain	Refreshment and new life.
Gate	An unexpected opportunity.
Gun	Discord, aggression, disaster, danger. ***Warning.***
Halo	Great spiritual virtue.
Hammer	Aggression. ***Warning.***
Harp	Angels are present, heavenly music, harmony, romance.
Hat	Honors, success. Can identify a particular person.
Hearth	A happy and protected home.
Heaven	Transcendence.
Helmet	Power, invincibility.

Herd

A group mentality, loss of independence.

Hexagram

Comprised of two interlocking triangles. Also known as the Star of David, Jewish symbol of mystical wisdom.
Symbolizes the union of male and female, of God and the soul.

Hive

Protection.

Horns

Male virility.

Horseshoe

Good luck if pointed up, but if down, disappointment.

Hourglass

Danger, time is running out. Be watchful of loved ones.

House

A real house. Look for identifying marks.
Also symbolizes your self-image, how you perceive yourself.

Jug

Caution against excess.

Key

A door will open, new opportunities.

Kite

Exaltation, direction, successful ambitions.

Knapsack

An unexpected journey. New beginnings.

Knife

Strife. ***Warning.***

Knot

A problem, internal or external.

Labyrinth

Symbolic journey to the underworld and back, of death and rebirth, an initiation.
Know how to remove yourself from a dangerous situation before entering into it.

Ladder

Gradual advancement.

Lamp

Discovery, enlightenment,
Dispels the darkness of ignorance.

Lemniscate   Mathematical sign of infinity.
The endless cycle of death and rebirth, of endless life.
Dominion, strength, control.

Letters   Letters of the alphabet are usually there for
identification purposes–a person, pet, etc.
Sometimes they form words or names.

Mandala   Symbolic image of the world, symbolic image of divinity,
and an aid to meditation.

Mask   Falsehood, deception.

Maze   See "Labyrinth."

Milky Way   The pathway of souls to the Otherworld.

Mirror   Reflects the true nature of things.

Mountain   If dark and cloudy, serious obstacles. If light and airy,
obstacles will be overcome.

Necklace   A gift. A bond between giver and wearer.

North Wind   Destructive powers.

Octagon   Resurrection and eternal life.

Ouroboros   A serpent biting its own tail symbolizes the circle (and
cycle) of eternity. The beginning and the end are one.

Parasol   Symbol of royalty and of heaven.

Pearl   Fertility, purity, love and marriage.

Pen   A writer.
Fate, or Destiny (It is written . . .")

Pentacle.   A five-pointed star. Magical symbol of the Wiccan and
other pagan religions.

Perfume   Sweetness, purity, virtue, a gift to the gods.

Pitchfork	Symbol of evil, of the devil.
Purse	Gain or loss. Examine surrounding images.
Question Mark	Caution required in all decision making.
Rainbow	A message of hope and the end of sorrow. A bridge to heaven.
Ring	Engagement or marriage.
River	Spiritual nourishment, emotional energy, the subconscious mind. Crossing a river in a boat can refer to a literal or symbolic death.
Rock	Stability, strength, permanence. If received as a gift from a spiritual source, the recipient has the gift of prophesy.
Rocket	The urge toward liberation and release from physical bondage.
Rods of Life	Fresh green branches symbolize health and energy.
Rope	Limitation, restriction, bindings, captivity.
Saint Andrew's Cross	Symbol of Scotland, after their patron Saint Andrew.
Scales	Justice is imminent. A possible lawsuit. If two scales, the sign of Libra.
Scallop Shell	Symbol of Venus, Goddess of Love. Love, beauty, feminine charm and sexuality.
Scarab	Egyptian beetle symbolizing life, death and rebirth.
Scepter	Authority, honors received.

Scissors	Quarrels, separation.
Scroll	A holy book, an injunction to follow God's law.
Scythe	Death of the physical body and freedom for the soul. ***Warning.***
Shield	Protection
Ship	A successful journey, increase by water. Study the ship's condition and surroundings.
Shirt	Protection.
Skull and Crossbones	Poisonous drugs. ***Warning.***
Spade	Hard work and successful results. If black, may indicate a death.
Star of David	See "Hexagram."
Stone	A symbol of wholeness. A place of worship.
Storm	A literal storm coming. A conflict.
Stream	A free flow of emotions. Healing energy.
Sun	Happiness and comfort, a new day, source of life. Creative power, energy, ambition, pride, leadership.
Sword	Strife, take quick action. ***Warning.*** Authority, strength, aggression, courage, war, destruction.
Teapot	Consultations, committee meetings.
Telescope	Discernment, adventure.
Temple	A holy place.

Tent	A shelter.
Tomb	Death, literal or figurative.
Tower	A sudden twist of fate which is designed to redirect the life upon its proper path.
Triangle	If apex is pointed up, good luck. If down, disappointment.
Trident	Symbol of Neptune, God of the Sea. Caution is advised if traveling by water.
Trumpet	Heralds a significant event.
Tunnel	A major transition is at hand.
UFO	A possible sighting.
Umbrella	If open, a shelter with friends. If closed, vexations. Rain in the forecast, be prepared.
Vase	Devoted service which brings reward. A treasure.
Volcano	A literal volcanic eruption. ***Warning.*** An emotional explosion. Find a constructive outlet for repressed anger.
Wand	Magic, psychism, power.
Water	Emotion, the unconscious, psychic energy. Mystery and the feminine.
Wavy Lines	Uncertainty, unsettlement.
Weapon	Conflict. ***Warning.***
Web	Intrigue. Beware of entrapment.

Wheel	Changes coming, the turn of fate.
Windmill	Industrious application will bring rewards.
Wings	Messages, transcendence.

Yin/Yang Change is cyclical. Within each cycle is the seed of the other. A wise person understands that for every thing there is a season, and adjusts accordingly.

BIBLIOGRAPHY

Andrews, Ted. *Animal Speak*. St. Paul, MN: Llewellyn Publications, 1995.

Ackroyd, Eric. *A Dictionary of Dream Symbols.* London: Blandford, 1993.

Bills, Rex E. *The Rulership Book.* Richmond, VA: Macoy Publishing & Masonic Supply Co., Inc., 1971.

Bruce-Mitford, Miranda. *The Illustrated Book of Signs & Symbols.* New York: DK Publishing, Inc., 1996.

Campbell, Florence. *Your Days Are Numbered.* Ferndale, PA: The Gateway, 1931.

Case, Paul Foster. *The Tarot.* Richmond, VA: Macoy Publishing Company, 1947.

Chevalier, Jean, and Alain Gheerbrant. *The Penguin Dictionary of Symbols.* London: Penguin Books, Ltd., 1996.

Ferguson, George Wells. *Signs and Symbols in Christian Art.* New York: Oxford University Press, 1954.

Heline, Corinne. *Sacred Science of Numbers.* Marina del Rey, CA: De Vorss & Co., Publishers, 1985 (sixth printing).

Jung, Carl G., et als. *Man and His Symbols.* London: Aldus Books Limited, 1964.

Jung, Carl G.. *Four Archetypes.* Princeton, NJ: Princeton University Press, 1970.

Leach, Maria, and Jerome Fried, eds. *Funk & Wagnalls Standard Dictionary of Folklore, Mythology, and Legend.* New York: Harper & Row, Publishers, Inc., 1984.

Levy, Judith S., and Agnes Greenhalls, eds. *The Concise Columbia Encyclopedia.* New York: Columbia University Press, 1983.

Matthews, Caitlin, and John Caitlin. *The Encyclopaedia of Celtic Wisdom.* Rockport, MA: Element Books, Inc., 1994.

Maynard, Jim. *Celestial Guide 1998.* Ashland, OR: Quicksilver Productions, 1998.

Sams, Jamie, and David Carson. ***Medicine Cards.*** Santa Fe, NM: Bear & Company, 1988.

The Asteroid Ephemeris, 1883–1999. Los angeles, CA: TIA Publications, 1977.

The Holy Bible. New York: Thomas Nelson & Sons, 1953.

Walker, Barbara G. ***The Woman's Encyclopedia of Myths and Secrets.*** San Francisco: Harper & Row, 1983.

Wasserman James. ***Art and Symbols of the Occult.*** Rochester, VT: Destiny Books, 1993.

Wilhelm, Richard, and Cary F. Baynes. ***The I Ching or Book of Changes.*** 3rd ed. Princeton, NJ: Princeton University Press, 1967.

ISBN 1-41205055-3